BUILDING
ON RIVER

BUILDING
ON RIVER POEMS

JEAN VAN LOON

Cormorant Books

Canada Council
for the Arts
Conseil des Arts
du Canada

ONTARIO ARTS COUNCIL
CONSEIL DES ARTS DE L'ONTARIO
an Ontario government agency
un organisme du gouvernement de l'Ontario

Canadian Patrimoine
Heritage canadien

The publisher gratefully acknowledges the support of the Canada Council
for the Arts and the Ontario Arts Council for its publishing program.
We acknowledge the financial support of the Government of Canada through the Canada
Book Fund (CBF) for our publishing activities, and the Government of Ontario through the
Ontario Media Development Corporation, an agency of the Ontario Ministry of Culture,
and the Ontario Book Publishing Tax Credit Program.

LIBRARY AND ARCHIVES CANADA CATALOGUING IN PUBLICATION

Van Loon, Jean, author
Building on river / Jean Van Loon.

Poems.
ISBN 978-1-77086-516-7 (softcover)

1. Booth, J. R. (John Rudolphus), 1827–1925 — Poetry.
I. Title.

PS8643.O549B84 2018   C811'.6   C2018-900034-1

Cover art and design: angeljohnguerra.com
Interior text design: Tannice Goddard, bookstopress.com
Printer: Sunville Printco

Printed and bound in Canada.

CORMORANT BOOKS INC.
10 ST. MARY STREET, SUITE 615, TORONTO, ONTARIO, M4Y 1P9
www.cormorantbooks.com

For Joan Harcourt
my travelling companion in the world of literature

Contents

J. R. Booth: A Brief Biography

John Rudolphus Booth arrived in roughhouse Bytown in the early 1850s with a wife, a child, and carpenter's tools bought on credit. After working for another man, building then managing his lumber mill, Booth went into business for himself. His first big contract was to supply lumber for the construction of the original Parliament Buildings. By the 1890s, his sawmill at the Ottawa River's Chaudière Falls was the largest in the world, employing 2000 in the mill and 4000 in the forests. He built an empire of forests, sawmills, pulp and paper mills, railroads, steamships and grain elevators. His life, 1827–1925, spanned the decline of the squared timber industry which had given life to Bytown, the rise and fall of the sawn lumber industry at the Chaudière, and the emergence of Ottawa as Canada's capital city.

He was a small man who loomed large, and not just in Canada. A tycoon who wore shabby clothing and workman's boots and laboured alongside his men. A stern patriarch with a wry sense of humour. A stubborn autocrat who fought against unionization, but delivered firewood to workers himself when fuel was short. A man conscious of every penny of business cost, but who hung hundred-dollar bills from the family Christmas tree and gave generously to charity. A man who had all his papers burned when he died.

Today, few know his story. The east-west freeway that cuts across Ottawa traces the former roadbed of his Canada Atlantic Railway. Yoga classes are offered on the site of his pulp and paper mills.

These poems are my attempt to imagine his life.

I

RIVER

Kichi Sibi

I spill from a world before words
into my names
    Kichi Sibi
      Adàwe
        La Grande Rivière
          Ottawa
            Outaoùais

from Lake Capimitchigama to Montreal
    through rapids, chutes and flats
      past mountains, peoples
          times

in spring I plunge like thunder
    range beyond my banks, sweep soil
      and rocks and branches from my path

summer-shrunk I purl
    in grassy bays of Lac des Chats
      and Lake Deschênes

winter binds me, surface stillness
    men may risk to trust
      under the ice my surges lurk

Sing the names of my sisters
    Camachigama   Chochouane   Capitachouane
      Mattawa   Petawawa   Madawaska
        Kipewa   Kinojéris   Wabi Creek
          Mississippi   Maganisipi   Temiskaming
        Lièvre   Blanquet   Bonnechère
      Petite Nation   Dumoine   Coulonge
  Rideau   Rigaud   Gatineau   Jocko
Blanche   Rouge   Noire
        forces twined, we grave our path

Here men felled forests once
raised mills

I shouldered their rafts, churned their turbines
                           drowned their devouring fires
            choked on their sawdust and refuse
                swallowed their calk boots
                   and their brothers

                                their buildings crumble
                    logs long gone

I flow on

2

A SHEFFORD LAD

Bytown, 1827

Into Lowertown ragged and randy
the shantymen ride the rivermelt
stinking of the camboose, craving
booze — and goose or moose or any food
that isn't beans with pork — calk boots
crammed with Bank of Montreal notes
from the winter's cut.
Hot-hearted Irish, gap-toothed fiddlers
sons of *habitants*, clog stompers
singers of *laisser passer les raftsmen*
they brawl for next year's work
and this week's whores
fly on ardent spirits
and high wines.

> Two hundred miles southeast
> in Lower Canada's Shefford Township
> on a stony homestead
> a second Booth son is born.

The Gillies, the Gilmours, the Brysons
pay no heed, nor the mighty Wrights.
Their timber rafts
          drift to Quebec City.
Anchored British bottoms
parch for cargo.

Shefford Township, Lower Canada

... A certain tract of Our waste land ... bounded on the north by a tract of Our waste lands commonly called the township of Roxton, on the south by the township of Brome, on the east by the township of Stukely, and on the west by a tract of Our waste lands commonly called the township of Granby ..."

— OFFICIAL REGISTRATION OF SHEFFORD TOWNSHIP, 1792

April 5, 1827

A raw wind laden with damp.
     Cold stone walls.
The mother hugs her new boy to her breast.

A runt, says the father. No matter. I'll teach him to work.

We'll call him John, she replies.

John Rudolphus. Let him grow into his name.

April, 1829

— Can you not make that child keep still? A man needs his rest.

— His eyes are like yours — blue that could cut through stone.

October, 1834

— Promise me you'll let him go to school. (She'll not rise again from this bed.) *He's so quick to learn.*

— His letters and numbers are all he'll need to farm.

J. R., Age Nine, Builds a Bridge

Runoff bulges the creek
a muscled river
if I look at it right, churning
alongside the field
icing my feet.

Yesterday's turtle
drags again onto its rock
head and legs outstretched
shell scarred. Midday sun
warms my shoulders.

I've cleared the brush
with the hatchet Father
made me. Now I can
spade the bank, anchor
a buttress shaped from

a fireplace log Father
must not notice missing
and the stump I dug out last week.
A dab hand with an axe, Mother said
now two years dead,

who told me Blue Flag
was the flower that looked like an iris
beside the summertime creek
who sweetened my sickbed
with a mug of wild roses.

A Schoolmaster Recollects ...

When he did attend
I had to look sharp.
If I turned my back
giggles spread around him —
solemn at his slate
when I whirled to see.

A clever lad
quick with his figures
a head for memory work.

Clinked the inkwell
shuffled his boots
raised his hand every day —
for the outhouse
he said. Took an outlandish time
even in glacial wind.

I put him in charge of the stove
to make good of his constant
motion. I must say
he knew how to tend it —
tossed in a split
just as the flame sank low.

Whispers in a Warm Fall Wind

J. R. versus Booth Sr.

The axe swings down and the wood splits
clean. I toss the pieces onto the rising pile.
Along the field edge the forest swells, as ever
it will, though we cut back each year.

> *He knows I'd gladly help him*
> *buy a farm. A good one's on offer*
> *scarce an hour's ride away*
> *thirty-eight acres cleared.*

If the farm were mine, I'd strip the slope
by the snye, build a mill
for shingles and planks. Damn
this mud. Boots braced in slick
I raise the blade.

> *Might as well preach to this stump. A farm*
> *yields bounty enough for a man and his kin —*
> *full bellies, a house built of stone. Not enough*
> *for J. R.'s stubborn bones.*

Beyond the heap of frost-sprung rocks
Brother James and Father rope
the next stump. The Percheron switches its tail.
My shoulders are stronger. James is older.

> *No dollar of mine will help him quit*
> *this place. You left Ulster, he argues.*
> *I arrived with five brothers.*

A warm wind freshens my temple. There was talk
after church of a railroad for central Vermont. Someone
will have to build trestles for all those ravines. The axe
swings down and the wood
splits clean.

Strange Stirrings in St. Armand

J.R. and Rosalinda

The inn was where I'd been told
and as I'd been told, respectable —
meals, a clean bed, stabling
for the stage's four-in-hand. All I could ask
halfway there, close to the border. Inside
dark, crackle of wood fire, tang of baking
bread — smells from my mother's stove.

> *One of the railway men*
> *stopping on visits home and back.*
> *Sat with the others to eat my mutton*
> *and dumplings. When he spoke*
> *men listened, laughed. His tipple*
> *was tea. When the drinkers grew loud*
> *and foolish, he lit a candle*
> *retired to his rest. With a nod*
> *to me. Like a gentleman.*
> *Up before dawn. Like me.*

I asked about the girl who served the dinner
and baked the bread. No girl, they said, a spinster gone twenty
not for a lad like you. Her face opened like dawn
when she looked at me. She was solid as maple
moved like a wisp of fog. *Rosalinda.* Honey on my tongue.

> *A well-made man with a stout head of hair.*
> *Could have done with a mend to his sleeve. Once*
> *he left a tip too large by half. For the view,*
> *he said when I told him, a teasing*
> *crease at the edge of his eyes. Blush*
> *flushed to the tips of my toes.*
>
> *Soft lips, supple — at least so they looked.*
> *He could have smiled, if he wished,*
> *from here to Montreal.*

I chose a chair that faced the kitchen door.
Each time she pushed out with a dish
I saw her first. When she gathered
the empty plates, apron strings
fingered her hips.

> *He asked where a man might buy a gift*
> *for his mother — leather gloves, perhaps,*
> *a bar of fine-milled soap. I lied*
> *and said I'd have to walk him there.*

> *Try the gloves for size, he said, if they don't fit you*
> *they won't do. The soap smelled of lavender.*
> *I smelled it as hard as I could*
> *all the way home. Beside him*
> *step by step. How could I have tricked*
> *an honest man? At the inn I confessed.*
> *My mother's long dead, he said.*
> *The soap's for you.*

I lingered till the last of the lads
had staggered to his cot. My work
is done come spring, I told her.
She dried the last flagon
again. I dragged my gaze
from her bosom to the fire.
I'll miss your dumplings
I said, breathing
deep

unless
you come with me.

> She folded
> the trembling towel.

Rosalinda's Road to Bytown

is river. Behind her, curve of stern
purl of wake. The steamboat's paddlewheels
sluice upstream, the sound almost

drowned by the chatter of passengers
shouts of two tattered boys. A whole day
for the voyage from Montreal, slowed

at each lock, Carillon, Chute-à-Blondeau, Long Sault.
Without benefit of cabin — twice the cost, he said. She brushes
wind-swirled soot from her first-born's brow.

J. R. paces, surveys the shoreline, asks the captain how much wood
the vessel burns, explains to Rosalinda how the locks were built
why the tugs and rafts, where that barge's cargo will be sold.

He's found a flat in a Mr. Fotheringham's house
Queen Street near the Bytown waterworks. Two rooms
he said, close to town as you asked.

Second storey, and she with a child to haul.
Stairs every in and out, to dump
the night-soil, hang the wash.

Left behind is the crate they've used as a table
the two pine boxes that served as chairs.   .
Better waits in Bytown, J. R. promised.

He points to Rideau Falls, McKay's gristmill, Barrack Hill.
A cliff breasts the river. Below it, another lock — mail cart,
teamsters, wagons, the rutted slope up to where they'll live.

Baby Gertrude, waked from her nap, squalls until he cradles
her crown in his palm. Her eyes widen and search —
child, Rosalinda knows, of a certain twisted-sheet night

her heart plunged into his hunger
    he into her shadows
        shadows and heat and an almost unbearable want.

My wife, he whispered
as if he could scarce believe it.

3

PINE LIKE GRASS FOR NUMBER

In Which Mayor John Scott Promotes Growth and Prosperity in Bytown

He surveys lots for mills
on Chaudière Island
woos American business with the power of the falls
and a promise.

Henry Franklin Bronson comes, with partner Harris
sawmill experience, contacts in the US lumber trade
and a nest egg.
No man bids against him. He pays
one shilling more than the fifty-pound floor.

William Goodhue Perley comes and partner Pattee
sawmill experience, contacts in the US lumber trade
and a nest egg. They buy a row of lots.
Unopposed.

John Rudolphus Booth comes from Shefford. No experience
in lumber exports. No contacts
in the trade. No nest egg. No favours
from John Scott.

No Godspeed from his father.

The Dream (in two versions)

J. R.

1. Chaudière, Spring Flood

Ice fog. Feeble early light.
I can scarcely see the road, but from my door
I hear the Chaudière roar, louder
with each stride toward my work.

From the bridge, at last I see the falls.
They hold me fast. Leamy and his mill
must wait. This rush.
This surge. A hefty timber

tossed by roiling swells. Runoff
funneled from the whole upper valley
plunges thirty feet, pounds the bridge
till it shivers, rumbles in my bootsoles.

I know every bolt
of Leamy's mill, will run it
when it's built. And well.
For wages.

Which I save. Soon I'll dare
a mill of my own, make this river
work for me. Another man's command
tastes like defeat.

2. High Water, 1854

The Ottawa plunges fierce through the Chaudière
thunders into foaming, tea-brown heaves.
Crossing Union Bridge, I slow and stare.

Ice fog, spray, rogue timbers toss to air.
I feel the torrents rage below my feet
riverwaters fierce through the Chaudière —

thrusting, thrashing forces — ripe to snare
so banks of saw-blade teeth slice pine sweet.
On Union Bridge, I ponder — do I dare?

My father said I'd fail if I strayed far
yet more each day Leamy trusts his mill to me.
Ceaseless, the river charges the Chaudière.

I'll not get rich on wages, even fair.
Another man's command tastes like defeat.
Crossing Union Bridge, I muse, prepare.

Someday I'll bow to no man. Leamy beware —
I'll build my own mill, bigger, and compete,
the river plunge for me at the Chaudière.
With Union Bridge my witness, this I swear.

Frances Gertrude

Rosalinda

1. Babe in the Wood

It won't always be this way
he swears, and tiptoes down the stairs   .
before daybreak, out through crisping
dark, across the misted river, gone
till nightfall. In the yard after supper
by kerosene lamp we make shingles. Profits
from waste wood, he says. His froe
splits as true as a knife cuts ham.
My draw knife dresses each shingle.
Gertrude curls a shaving around her thumb.

We've both known babies — younger brothers
and sisters for him and for me. None like
our Frances Gertrude: the sleek of her skin
scent of her hair, the way she calms
at his voice. While I bathe her
he makes shadow puppets. They wobble
with the flame. When she laughs
all three of us do.

She's smart like her papa
wears me out with her climbing,
can't stay away from the staircase.
Barely two, she speaks like a child
of three. I talk to her all day.

2. Wildfire

His workday done, face gaunt
he asks, is she improved?
The sheets and diapers I've boiled
hang in the room to dry, rice-water by her crib

and a jar of Leibig's Essence of Meat.
Her wee face is damp and rashed, shorn scalp
wrapped in cooling cloths. Scarlet Fever,
the doctor said, ulcers in her throat.
His tonic smells of ammonia.
She will not take it.

John willingly pays the doctor's fee,
though he vaunts rhizome of Mayapple's
proven worth. He tries shadow puppets.
Gertrude turns away.

3. Ashes

Condolences do not soothe.
Nor John's bony body
beside me at St. Andrew's.
I feel his shakes.

At home, a tear spits on the stove
as I make tea. Before I can pour
he stands at the top of the stairs
in working clothes,
one knee a-twitch. I need
to be at the mill, he says.

The chair where I nursed her
is cold and hard. No warming
weight on my shoulder. No squeals
follow a ball around the floor.
I can't even press my face
into her clothes — burned
with the toys.

A Letter from Shefford

J. R.

I shouldn't have opened it.

Why write me of our insalubrious air
the grippe that afflicts
every winter, the cholera, typhoid,
diphtheria, whooping cough. Those
did not drain her light.

Besides, I live on the hillside,
well above the river flats
far from Lowertown's boggy exhalations.
And so I have told him.

Yes, his farm air is pure. Yes,
his children thrive. But what about
my mother? Would I tell him
she shouldn't have died?

He could have written of sorrow.

Sneak Thief

J. R.

Slowly and out of sight it takes hold.
Spark from metal on metal?
Worker's furtive pipe?

Consuming one board, it heats the next
ready to flick into flame, light visible
only in dark, smoke seen only
when fire has firmed its grip.

Lost thus, the mill I rented from Leamy,
my first, that made lath from scrap.
Thus, the mill rented from Thompson,
boards in process, my equipment for cutting
and handling, my letterbook copies
of business missives.

Thus, acres of forest.

Smoke's sting
the only warning.

Sheltered by wood, my family sleeps.
I rise in the dark. Sniff.

Remembering Shefford

J. R.

— kicks and coughs
shared bed and body heat
whines of the weanling, cries of the newborn
shards of summer light, mean breath of breeze
the trudge to school through gunshot woods of winter

— how Father could afford
a large stone farmhouse
blacksmith shop
lodge for the Orange Order
only the meanest schooling for his children

— Mother's chapped hand guiding mine to the garden weeds
scent of apple blossom, lilac and hydrangea
copper glow of lilies in late-day sun
and then, her rippling voice gone.
I but seven years old.

— the lash of Father's words
weight on my back of a winter's flour and lard ·

— stench of barns burning — *Les Patriotes* —
corn and potatoes shredded by vicious hail
wheat rust, snow in June

No man controls his fate by owning a farm.

Pennies Count

J. R.

Outside, the darkened street
not far from the escarpment
soon to be Parliament Hill. Mine
the single bright window

kerosene flame at my desk. Columns
of calculations march my page. Three
government buildings. Years of steady money
ride on this tender. And my name.

I'll scrap the tradition of oxen
save with horses, bring in idle longshoremen
from Montreal, bellies pinched
and gnawing from months on strike.

Rosalinda quilled like a porcupine
when I said I would bid.
They'll give it to one of their own, she said.
What if horses prove they can't draw the weight?

I allow myself to imagine —
well-barbered faces fall
the brimming cup of fortune
snatched by an upstart.

Where will you get the capital?
asked Rosalinda. Where will you find the trees?
All I'll need is the contract. Bankers will joust
for my custom. Woodlot owners will slaver.

She stands in the doorway now, a flow
of white flannel. It's past three, she says
you've only two hours to sleep. Swaying folds.
Softness underneath. I blow the room dark.

The Bid is In

Rosalinda

In the dark his arm trembled
under my breasts, over the round
of the coming child. A third
to feed, fluttering
like my heart.

I topped his bony forearm with my own
fingered the wrist-knob, bare, spare

turning, held him
tobacco-breath, beard-scratch, drowning man's clutch
pump, press, release.
And then we slept.

Morning woke me.
He was gone.

J. R.

Water rush. Clap of sawn wood
slapped onto a wagon. Men
shout. Gears growl.
My wall clock
ticks.

Perched on my office stool
I busy myself with letters.
Whatever the outcome
this mill will rumble.
I've other customers.

When I can bear the wait no more
I join the men at the wagons
in the joy of bend
and heave, the sweetness
of pine and horses.

Working the Limit

Booth's shanty boys

black spruce   balsam   prime white pine
a harvest waits
stinging day and a span of bays
we sledge the snows of the swamper's trail
broadaxe   canthook   jammer rope
prize trunks crash
tops lopped   sides hewn
we strew the slash
tops lopped   sides hewn
prize trunks crash
broadaxe   canthook   jammer rope
we sledge the snows of the swamper's trail
stinging day and a span of bays
a harvest waits
black spruce   balsam   prime white pine

Spring Drive

creek-ice cracks
    puddles spread

river drivers lace their calks   wield
     peaveys   topple
        the 50-foot brow of a skid
           pole the sticks into rising rush
up to their thighs
  in ice water

they burl through roar   steer
   logs downstream leap
     from the sinking land
on the floater   climb
           high on logjams   pry
    the key log
        free

tributes along the route   boots
nailed crosswise to trees
boots of men who broke a jam
     and broke

Over Port, the Manager of the Bank of British North America Recounts the Auction of the Egan Timber Limits

Two hundred fifty square miles of virgin pine.
Of course, the Crown chose a recession
to market the rights. If they'd taken advice ...
if they'd waited five years ...

Booth, with no ready cash, came to see me.
We're both of the Scotch Church, you see. Till then
he'd financed everything himself — with what,
you'd wonder, seeing the mends on his coat.

I asked, as required, what he'd offer
in way of security. Up came his fists
and down they slammed on my desk.
These, he said.

Hands tendoned and tough, but it was the eyes
that made me say aye. Blue like an iceberg
diamond-sharp, with a glint. I'll bid nothing,
he said, till I've heard from my timber cruiser.

We walked to the auction directly, in drizzle, Sparks
Street stinky-slick with mud. In the drawing room
of the Russell House Hotel, the air was spiced with cigar
every inch of the carpet covered by standing men's boots.

Mclaren was there, and Gillies, Gilmour most likely
too, though I didn't see him. Reporters, loiterers
the curious. We'll stand here, said Booth
planted near a doorway and a half-filled spittoon.

Like a mustang in a corral, he was.
Without the space to pace.
He scanned the assembly. Pulled
out his watch: gone a quarter of.

I offered a cigar.
He tucked a plug into his cheek.

Where's Robert? he muttered.
Pembroke's not that far away.
Damn his hide!

The auctioneer set his gavel on the lectern, and a man
popped up beside us, damp wool smell, haste-flushed
face. He bent to Booth and whispered: pine like grass
for number, quality unexcelled, pay any price.

$45,000

J. R.

I rein in the rented dray, and the wagon stops. But for the beast's
steamy snorts, all is still. As far as I can see, white pine
and red, trunks the girth of a table. Mast-straight.

All of Ottawa gibbers about the vast sum I paid.
The storied Egan limits are mine —
two hundred fifty square miles of nothing but trees.

I jump from the wagon onto the forest floor,
rust-red in the late-day light, bend a bundle
of needles, suck in the piney scent.

Poll axes will whack their bites, rude men will shout,
heartwood crack and topple — millions of board feet
year after year. Squared logs, deals, and dollars.

The year's first snowflakes settle like sawdust
over the mare's dun rump. Time to turn homeward.
But not for a moment, yet.

Tale of the Camboose Shanty Boy

I was fifteen my first winter up for Booth.
Worked as cookee. Seventy cents a day
cash pay come spring. Men's work.

The shanty was new when I got there,
smelled of fresh-cut pine. A skinny man
ground an axe on the stone inside the door.
Sharp enough to shave a man, he said.

I rang the wake-up bell
at half past four, cut slices of long clear pork
for the cook, picked through beans
for fifty men. In the evening I peeled spuds,
so tired I could hardly grip the knife.

We kept the door closed against cold,
all our light and air from the roof hole
over the camboose sandpit.
Night and day, that fire beat out heat,
Cook and I as smoked as kippers.

Outside, upwind, the cold smelled
like bedsheets dried in sun.
I was glad to go on errands
to cutting crews — fellers

who placed a falling trunk as sure
as I leaned the broom against a wall,
hewers whose broadaxes
smoothed a squared-off timber
soft as my baby sister's skin.

We slept in double-decker bunks, mine
a "muzzle-loader" jammed in on both sides.

I had to climb over the foot
to join the big lad snoring there before me.

I listened to bedtime knives stab the wall,
someone chop tobacco grown back home,
one more blade scrape across the whetstone.
Those nights, sleep swallowed me.

By Christmas, smoke had soured the walls.
We breathed sulfur farts and rancid hair, filthy
socks and underdrawers. Some of the lads
had spots from "logger's smallpox" —
                    boot spikes, poker fights.

But Saturday nights — lilting fiddle
steady thump of boots on the shanty floor.
I couldn't help but show my step-dance too.
When we sang "The Jam on Gerry's Rock"
about the drowning of young Monroe
men cried.

Those tall tales I tell? Mufferaw Joe? The Flying Canoe?
Those were from Sundays.
Raisin pie and time to smoke a pipe.

Some mornings I went out in the dark
to watch the teamsters feed and hitch the horses.
Canned daylight licked from oil-filled tins.
Quick-handed men
       frost-breathing beasts
              clink of trace chains.
Flickers
on the snow.

Raftsmen

"I was amazed to see floating down the stream a most gigantic raft, with some 30 or 40 wooden houses upon it and at least as many flag staffs, so it looked like a nautical street."
— CHARLES DICKENS, DESCRIBING A SHIPMENT OF TIMBER PASSING ALONG THE ST. LAWRENCE RIVER TOWARD CARGO SHIPS AT QUEBEC IN 1842.

Two thousand timbers to our raft, cargo its own craft.
    Our floating village whispers down the lake
white sails sagged, without a thin wind's breath.
    Fiddle stilled, men snore toward toilsome day.

As our floating village slips along the lake
    cook fire dances in the camboose, sleep-shanties cast shadows.
With fiddle stilled, toilsome men snore toward the day
    clothing soaked. Spills and splashes — will we ever dry?

Cook fire dances in the camboose, sleep-shanties cast their lines.
    Like me, some twenty men wear clothing soaked
by spills and splashes. We will never dry.
    Awake, we'll break our raft to narrow cribs.

Some twenty men like me snatch soaking rest before
    we ride the timber slide to skirt the falls.
The raft in narrow sections — one by one
    a hundred cribs sluice downstream

along the timber slide and past the falls.
    Stiff fingers numb with cuts
we gather the hundred cribs one by one
    yoke them tight, rebuild our raft.

Numb fingers stiff with cold
    sweeps jammed in corner oarlocks
we steer our rebuilt raft
    through tides and currents.

The sweeps in corner oarlocks
    veer our craft from ragged rocks
my two cousins pitch into tide and currents.
    We kneel, mourn young souls lost

two swept against ragged rock by torrents.
    In Quebec City's coves, pay and harbour.
Mourning lost mates, we fold sails,
    load the battered hulks of square-rigged droghers.

Here in Quebec City's crowded harbour
    white sails sag, without a thin wind's breath.
We feed our vessel-cargo into droghers.
    Two thousand timbers. Raft a craft no longer.

After Harvest

dumb stumps

           a homeless raven's crrr-a-a-a

     trees not fit   .

tinder

Glimpsed at Forty

What small man is this who strides the shadows
of dawn's road — rough coat, cloth cap
tradesman's boots mud-laden

alert at this hour of ghosts with baker
teamster, tavern keeper readying bread and beer
the watchman who tips his cap at the sawmill gate?

Family Portrait 1869

J. R.

It was worth buttoning into my starched shirt.
Rosalinda bowed my tie, insisted I brush my beard.
Now I'm preserved on film, presiding

over my family. Gertrude and Lila swathed
in new dresses — pleated flounces and fancy sleeves —
ringlets, hair ribbons, shiny boots.

The boys on the floor dressed like the little men they are
Jackson strict at six, Frederick bored at four. My right arm
extends as if to defend Rosalinda's chair

her kind face sober, hair severe. In black
for little Frank, gone just this year, not
two years old. Three children lost. Maybe

my father is right about tainted air.
No. This photo will show him:
my family's hale. I'm doing well.

The Weaver's Tale

—found poem

The saw on his left
sets the pace. If the singing blade
rips 50 rough shingles
off the block every minute
the sawyer must reach over
to its teeth
50 times in 60 seconds;
if the automatic carriage
feeds the odorous wood 60 times
into hungry teeth, 60 times
he must reach over, turn the shingle, trim its edge
on the gleaming saw in front of him
cut the narrow strip containing
the knot hole with two quick movements
and toss the completed
board down the chute
to the packers,
                              meanwhile
keeping eyes and ears open
for the sound that asks him
to feed a new block into untiring teeth.
Hour after hour the shingle weaver's
hands and arms, plain, unarmored
flesh and blood, staked against
the screeching steel that cares not
what it severs. Hour after hour the steel
sings its crescendo as it bites
into the wood, the sawdust cloud
thickens with fine particles.

Sooner or later he reaches
a little too far, the whirling blade
tosses drops of deep red
into the air, and a finger, a hand
or part of an arm comes sliding
down the slick chute.

A Tale of Sawdust

I.

In quiet shallows
below the Chaudière, sunlit water
bark-tinted, clear.

A school of silver minnows
drifts and darts, glimmers
through ripples.

2.

All day long, rotating chains
draw logs up jackladder troughs
into Chaudière mills.

The slabber gate shears off
rough outsides, gang saws
slice the core into boards,

circular saws trim away flaws.
Boys, paid children's wages,
pick out prime trimmings

to sell for shade rollers, lath or fuel,
butt-ends to make into matches.
The rest is waste. Wagonloads

in the darkness of night
dumped into the river — blocks
chips, bark — and sawdust.

3.

Above the swimming minnows
a shadow darkens, swirls
down through the water

smothers the spawning grounds.
A shoal grows river-wide
laden with sawmill debris.

4.

M. Ratté owns a boat-house
taxis passengers from Ottawa
to Hull, rents out rowboats.

Mill waste thickens the river.
M. Ratté's boathouse
fills, its entrance clogged.

He sues the mill owners.
Wins. They pay fat fines.
And keep on dumping.

Daybreak scullers
struggle. Debris
cumbers their oars.

5.

In the river's depths, sawdust rots.
Sends out wafts of stink.
Gas bubbles form and grow.

6.

Downstream, off L'Orignal
a fisherman lets his rowboat drift
lines out for *barbotte*.

Below the boat, sawdust.
A methane bubble, trapped
by layers above, expands and swells

until the shoal explodes. Tossed
from the capsized craft, the fisherman
lands unconscious, face down. Bubbles rise

from his jacket sides. His boots
fill with water. River
closes over his head.

7.

A Select Committee
of Parliament's Senate
convenes to hear complaints:

> *An explosion one night blew up 60 feet of the ice*
> *right on the road. If any teams had been there,*
> *they would have been lost.*

> *I live right over the cliff, see sawdust come down the river*
> *three explosions a week in front of my house,*
> *a barge thrown up clear of the water.*

> *Before, every eddy was full of fish*
> *pickerel pike black bass and mascalonge*
> *now you might fish a week and not catch two*

When the forest is gone, says Sir John A.
we'll restock the river with fish
at government cost.

8.

The government sets rules.
Most mill owners obey. Booth
stalls. Fined, he pays the $20.

Stalls again until he's ready
to invest. A new mill for pulp.
Another to make paper.

He sells his waste
as pages
for the *New York Times*.

9.

In 1951, Princess Elizabeth will cruise the Ottawa.
A lady reporter — stepping, she thinks, ashore —
will sink through debris to the bottom.

Engineers of the 1960s, preparing footings
for the Macdonald-Cartier bridge
will dig into sawmill waste three metres deep.

Why a Turtle?

asks son Jackson
when you show him your symbol
on the bark.

> To show the timber's mine.

But why a turtle?
Because it lives by the river?
Because slow and steady wins the race?

> To make little boys ask questions.

Because turtles live long lives? asks Rosalinda.
Because they wear a dark, plain suit?

> To make grown women ask questions.
>
> You hold the axe like this, blaze
> an oval fourteen inches long. See —
> four straight cuts make legs.
> Quick and easy.

No poetry in your bones. Not a grain.
The turtle nothing to do with the smell of mud
in the creek back home
or the carapace between you
and those who look down on you.

Your First New House

Frances Gertrude, dead at two, never sees it. Nor Augusta Adella,
      dead at five. Nor Frank, who lives but sixteen months.
Rosalinda waits for it twenty-one years.

Stone the grey of ripening summer clouds
      chimneys graceful as birch trees, gables, dormers, spires.
You plant apple trees, maples, hydrangea — a perfect young pine.

You set it on Wellington Street, within sight of your Chaudière mills.
      Not New Edinburgh, with the McKays
and Keefers, private school privilege, university degrees.

North winds slice across the flats, scour your pillared
      porches and flowerbeds ribboned with paths,
shake the twinned bedroom windows with rounded tops.

I picture you with the architect, in your rented Bridge Street home.
      You'd no more give him his head than the horse
you drive to your forests or the men who labour there.

A bedroom for every child, you insist. Four, and one more coming.
      A study for you — fit to receive Sir John A.
A room for Rosalinda's curved-leg writing table.

Matched in stubborn wills, you and the architect huddle,
      pipe smoke curling above the table lamp's chimney.
You call for tea. Splashes from the kitchen pump,

kettle-clank onto the stove. Pull up a chair for me, Rosalinda says.
      Cups rattle into saucers. Who do you think
will spend all day in the place?

May Belle, your youngest, will play and grow
      in this house, born the year you move in,
adored as "Chum." Gertrude and Lila

will float down the fine oak staircase in wedding silk.

      Frederick brush dark shoulders for his marriage. Rosalinda
burn with her last pneumonia, Chum with fatal TB.

At bedtime, did you follow your watchman's lantern —
      dot of light among towering lumber stacks?
Did your windowpane glow red when the Great Fire neared?

Glimpsed at Fifty

Who is this who stops the saws mid-shift
re-sets a trimming edge, remarks the newest
horse to join the fleet, strokes its cheek

greets by name a customer not seen
these last twelve years, jumps into a pit
to help a struggling carpenter hoist a beam?

Tea on the Verandah: In Which Rosalinda Reports to Her Lady Friends on the Trip to Atlantic City

It was the girls who heard about it, at Miss Harmon's ...

Sugar?

the sea, the boardwalk, the fashions —
between you and me and the gatepost
they didn't mention fashions to their father.
The boys could build sandcastles, they said
the girls would watch over them by the water.

Lila baked these cookies
this morning, Sand Dollars.
Isn't that just the thing?

The girls talked without let about needing a taste of sea air,
how Ottawa smelled of wood smoke and horse manure.
Such language from young ladies! And what did they know
of sea air, though I must say it did sound appealing.

You know Booth. A new turbine to see to.
He had to talk to a man about a barge.

Gertrude mentioned a flower show, under glass,
growers from all across the USA — I swear his ears
clicked open. He tends all the flowerbeds around this house
by himself, keeps me in bouquets well into the fall
from the bed of yellow chrysanthemums over there.

Warm your cup?

It was train to Montreal, where Booth had a day of business.
Train again from there. On the bridge at the St. Lawrence

I almost took a turn, the water below dark and flowing fast.
Gertrude looked to her guidebook for the sights. Lila —
oh my! how she chattered! When the boys took a notion
to race up and down the aisles, I had to pry Booth
from his paper to make them stop.

>Gertrude, dear, would you please
>pass the cookies?

We checked into a lovely boardwalk hotel. By the time
the boys were settled, I had no trouble at all falling asleep.

In the morning, Booth was down in the lobby.
I've been out since half past five, he said, and seen
what there is to see. The rest of you can stay. I'm going home.

Death of the Old Man

J. R.

At the establishment of the purveyor of gravestones

I want your best red granite
fine-grained and polished to shine
carved plain. John Booth. With his dates.
And my mother's. Eleanor Rowley Booth.
And those of his second wife.
And the children who died before him.

Yes, a big one. No matter the markets are dull.
Pack it with care. It must travel to Shefford —
train and then miles by coach.
I'll take it myself.

On the stage coach

This ride is why I visited seldom.
Shakes a man's brain from his head
even now when the road is dry —
rock-pocked, deep-ditched, rutted.

The route you refused to travel, though I offered
a generous room and meals you'd not taste at home.
The harvest needed you, or the livestock
or one of the children — none of them children long since.

I'd have shown you through each of the mills. The timber
slide, the upper river. And the house, stone
like yours but five times the size, with plentiful
windows, scrollwork trim, gardens on every side.

If you'd had your way, none of it would have been.
Your dreams were wide enough to let yourself fly
but not me.

You'll be nothing if you don't start with land
you said. What family have you in Bytown?
If you go, don't beg to me in your time of need.

I never begged. Who else of your thirteen
children could bring such a stone
as rides in a luxury crate on this coach?

At the graveside

— Don't be beholden.
— Never spend more than you must.
— Enough work is never enough.

Always I heard your voice.
When I won the contract to supply
the parliament, I pictured your face.

The stone is my tribute to you.
As strong. As hard. As cold
as now you lie

and I wish you did not.
I've more to show you.

4

IN THE THICK

In Which J. R. Sets Himself on Track

Fireflicker echoes in the walnut
of Rosalinda's chair
catches a crimp of hairpin
in her tugged-back bun. She stretches
mottled wool over the wooden egg.

> What did you do to your mitt? Looks
> gnawed by a rat.

>> *American Lumberman* rustles page to page
>> in J. R.'s hasty hands.

>>> come freeze-up everything stopped ... months
>>> barges ... load unload ... every minute a dollar

You'll have to speak up if you want me to hear.

>>> too slow ... too damned slow ...

Her darning needle glints through the warp.

> I'm working as fast as I can.

Fire snaps. Sparks rise and vanish.
Rosalinda snips the yarn.

>> a good 800 miles shorter

>> *American Lumberman* swishes onto the red
>> Turkey carpet.

> I mean to build my own railway.

A silver sliver stops mid-air.

> But you've always said ...

>> And I mean to not lose money.
>> Damned if my freight
>> will fill another man's pocket.

Coteau Landing to Ottawa

— *September 11, 1882*

Locomotive 10 spits pretty
near the shore of the St. Lawrence. Steam
curls round her shiny black sides.
Her smokestack's tall and funneled
tender piled with firewood, cattle
catcher fanned like ladies' skirts.

Fine-suited guests climb Pullman steps
removing hats to ooo and ah
at the carpet, swivel armchairs
and the fine brass lamps.
She whistles and they're moving,
bunting all a-flutter, and she gathers
speed so quickly soon the river's
far from sight.

Twenty-five and thirty, then forty
miles an hour, opening up to sixty
on a perfect stretch of straight
she streaks through fields and fallow
swampy poplar, cedar scrub, riding
steel rails and spruce sleepers laid
on ballast tamped down hard.

With well-stuffed seats and panelled walls
what a party does she carry!
Directors of the board, Mayor
St. Jean and legislators
cigars and — who knows — whiskey?
Through Saint-Polycarpe, Glen Robertson
Maxville and Moose Creek,
Casselman, Limoges, and Carlsbad Springs.

Approaching Ottawa, she slows,
crosses the canal bridge, pulls up beside
the new frame station, Catherine Street at Elgin.
The men stub smokes. Steel wheels screech
and steam exhales. The Canada Atlantic has arrived.

Booth salutes the parting guests
turns to partner Perley:
there's still the damn St. Lawrence in the way.
A ferry's fine to start
but it's sure to be too slow
we need that God-damn bridge from Coteau.

J. R. Bridges the Gap: Federal By-Election 1887

J. R.

Sir John A. stands in Renfrew dust
surrounded by lusty woodsmen
who want to meet Old Tomorrow.
He asked me to join his campaign
here — my forests near. My chance
for his ear.

I tell him I don't see his problem, the government
bounty part of my railway charter, I merely
the man who at last delivered the span
across the St. Lawrence.

> He shakes the hand
> of a rough and ruddy supporter.

> Ferguson needs to win,
> he tells me, clasps his hands
> behind him, bends
> to attend a petitioner.

Good man, I say. Runs
my business for all this zone.

> His fingers rub a thumb.

My support flows forth
in words from campaign platforms
streams as paper money hand to hand
floats Ferguson to victory.

Political partner Perley
arrives early at my office door.
The bounty is ours.

Making Tracks to Georgian Bay

J. R.

I slow the span of blue roans —
corduroy at the farm lane's swampy mouth —
harness clinks
rattling wagon.

On the road
as when I left my father's farm
to muscle trestles
for the Central Vermont.

A horse lifts its tail — a golden
thud lands in the dirt, a pleasant smell soon lost
in the fragrance of woodlot
ripening hay.

The rutted lane opens.
I could be back in Shefford — meagre
clearing wrenched from forest
a farmhouse that leaks ragged children.

My muscles, stiff from sitting
ache for the strains of the farmer
who trudges from a stubborn stump
rough sleeve blotting his reddened brow.
Might I give you a hand? I ask.

Job done, the two of us rest
at the kitchen table. Tea. Bread —
with butter, for a guest. Patched
pot on the stove. I need
a right of way, I tell him.
I pay cash.

Two more farms along the road
then a bed at the stopping place. Tomorrow

on to the next — barking dog, house
weathered dark, enclosing
what bruises, what fractured dreams.

Cash is a salve.

Terminus: St. Lawrence to Georgian Bay
J. R.

I squint before the inland sea my piers
will probe despite the town,
see swells my steamers will plow, holds
swollen with joists and purlins

for Chicago, Milwaukee, Duluth
hulls on return groaning with grain,
spices of Asia, Australian wool,
rails from here to the eastern seaboard.

To hell with Parry Sound, shore lands
amassed in grasping hands.
I march south — sand coves,
chatter-chipped granite.

Parry Island, an easy span across the bay
nineteen thousand acres
a few rough cabins.
God's own harbour.

Reserve of Ojibwa, Odawa, and Pottawatami
land I can buy under law
for railway use.

*

Beyond the bounds of the severed
land, the Parry Island band.
Inside, I build

a rail bridge to a town I name Depot Harbour
wharves and water towers, elevators for two million
tons of grain, bunk house, offices, school, churches

of every Christian hue.
One hundred new houses for white workers
come for the railroad jobs.

... At the residence of her husband ... Rosalinda, beloved wife
of J. R. Booth

> *Lamented lady ... Worthy lady ...*
> *a quiet and uneventful domestic life ...*

Not for you
his home remedies. Two
doctors pressed trained
fingers to your blazing
brow, bowed
to your rattling breath.

> *fell a sleep in death ...*
> *departed ...*
> *deceased ...*

At your funeral five
preachers presided. Eight
prominent pallbearers knew
lumber, railways, markets
and your husband. Two hundred sixty-eight
carriages crawled in cortège.

> *in consequence of the sad event*
> *the firm mills at the Chaudière*
> *will remain closed until after the funeral*

You stirred laundry at the boil
in icy rented houses, hands
lye-cracked, eyes wood-smoked

you chopped rutabagas
scrubbed soot, beat carpets, fetched
a plumber to fix the frozen drain

washed small lifeless bodies, tender Frances
Gertrude, Augusta Adella's flower-stem neck
toddler Frank's cowlick slicked to stay.

Your photo shows a gold-chained watch
like his. Please tell me he gave it to you
because he knew the labours of your days.

His floral tribute a pillow labeled: Mother. Please
tell me when he reached for you at night
he called you Rosalinda. Rose.

In St. Andrew's Presbyterian
stained glass in your memory
your name misspelled Rosalind.

Who sent the tribute in anchor shape?
Why did someone send a Maltese Cross?
Whose were the small cut-flower bouquets?

He closed all mills for five full days.

Family Tree

J. R.

Your family is here in Shefford
my father said, fierce against Bytown.

Rosalinda hinted about sister Letitia's husband.
I hired him.

Rosalinda whispered of sister Martha.
I found her man a job.

Rosalinda broached the subject of her brothers.
Thomas ... and Albert and James — I engaged them all.

Cousin Robert from Pembroke — he who appraised
    the Egan Limits —
married Rosalinda's sister Victoria.

Nephews and grand-nephews nursed ambitions in the shanties.
Cousins in Montreal chased customers.

My father put forward E. J. Booth, youngest son, by his second wife.
At last, I said. And hired him.

In Rosalinda's cortège, twenty-two carriages of family.

Rainy May in the J. R. Booth House

J. R.

her black skirts swish past my deaf side

velvet crushed on the seat of her lady's chair

her eyes red-rimmed in Chum's swollen face

cook asks *me* whether beef or mutton

closet empty but for her scent, crammed shirtwaist box in the cellar

her firm footfall on the step

silver-backed brush with a long grey hair

rattle of her watch chain on the marble-top commode

hairpins like Hansel's breadcrumbs leading   nowhere

bedsheets chill on my skin

at the mill men shout belts rumble steel wheels screech

she's not dead there

Rainy August

J. R.

When I open the door after work
Chum stands lost in the empty hall
a well-dressed waif. As if I could redress

what's missing. Am I to guide a young girl
into womanhood? My other daughters
long grown and gone, Gertrude

with children of her own, Lila
abroad. Chum shadows me
as I drain my umbrella and glance

at the newspaper headline. A hug
is a mother's province. Yesterday
I told her a joke. And she laughed.

Trips to meet customers, meetings
of corporate boards will take me away
night after night.

She stands by my chair as I open
The Globe, chatters to me as I read. Her face
the shape of Rosalinda's. Rosalinda's eyes.

There are fine boarding schools
in Toronto. I'll send her there.
I cannot bear it.

Mending

J. R.

Welcome, Uncle J. R.
The front door opens wide
my nephew summons his mother.

I shrug off coat and scarf
lean my cane on the oak hall tree
tender these tattered mitts

the last pair knit by Rosalinda.
Her sister sits — same hitch
of her hips, arm-twitch, darning

egg, needle-gleam, weave, female
chatter of distant cousins, fire —
I melt into the chair.

Chum Writes from School

J. R.

Dear Papa

    I hate Toronto.

★

    The teacher is mean
    and the food is horrid.
    The bed has no quilt.
    Nobody likes me.

★

    Yesterday
    somebody stole
    my thaumatrope.
    I tore my dress
    when they made me
    jump rope in the yard.
    I don't feel well.
    I need to be at home.

★

After school I could go to Gertrude's and
        help with the baby or I could stay with Lila or
visit with Auntie Letitia or Auntie Martha and
        Nurse could fix my dress and
            you could help me string a new thaumatrope
I miss you
        and Frederick and Jackson
            and my sweet little Bunnie and Elsie at school
and all of the horses especially Mamselle Bones

I promise to eat my porridge
and tidy my room
and draw quietly while you are working
I won't touch your papers
I'll go to bed without asking. I really don't feel well
please please please
let me come home.

Chum Comes Home

J. R.

Skin thin on bone
eyes wide
with why

TB of the lungs, said Doctor Wright

— he started at my stare —

she could have caught it
here.

Phthisis
Phthisis pneumonalis
Consumption.
I shall buy all
the books.

Papa, she said
sit with me.

White Plague

J. R.

So many names for it. Scientists
have noted its several varieties. Dr. Kock
says it spreads by infection.

Still no cure. Five years
they say she'll last.
I mean to do better:

the frailest flower can thrive
tended in shelter.
Dr. Trudeau at Saranac Lake

proposes bed rest, rich food,
fresh winter air. But the child needs
company. My body resists

sitting. It feels to me idle
though she loves to hear me read
even from business reports.

Jackson pronounced my prescription:
take your skis. Clean manly sport
in invigorating air — then to her porch

she shrouded in mounds of quilts
I in winter wool coat and lap robe,
colour in both of our cheeks.

May Belle's View from the Cure Cottage, Saranac Lake

Your ski tracks
cross empty white
outside cold glass

side by side as close
as you and I in the days
when you called me Chum

and I felt precious
in your eye, ice-blue turned melt
when bent to me.

When you packed me away
to school I stole
a photo from poor Mama's

commode, me six years old
my lace-hemmed dress
your gentleman's chair

your trousers raspy wool
pine and cigar, thick fingers
gripping our book.

J. R. Looks Back

She made it to twenty-three.
Well above the five-year forecast.
I tried my best, kept up with the research
studied the latest treatments into the night

took her myself to Saranac Lake
for Dr. Trudeau's winter cure
built a cure cottage at Kingsmere
for her summers.

She never blamed me.
The flush of her cheeks
fixed me deeper in shame
than if she had.

When I slipped into talk of work
she surprised me
with what she knew. Some errors
cannot be corrected.

Fire Trains

— April 26, 1900

A stovepipe reddens
    against a thin wood wall
        that rises to a roof with wooden shingles
           same as the houses that stand
           shoulder to shoulder
                working men's houses
        morning, north-side Hull
within the hour, several blocks ablaze.

Noontime crowds line the cliff at Parliament Hill
        to watch Hull burn
           as three times before.

High winds from the North hurl firebrands
    roof
        to roof
           to riverside stacks of sawn lumber
                eight times the height of a man
        planks stacked in layers to dry
           with air between
              furnace-hot
    pine resin feeding ravenous flame
skies glowering red
        one stack then the next
           like cars of a train.
        Fire trains, says Senator Clemow on the cliff.

Trains that lead to the Chaudière Bridge
        mills lining both sides across to Ottawa
Eddy's, Bronson's, Hull's, the power plants of Ottawa Electric

and Booth's sawmill, largest in the Empire
its barges and steamers at anchor

500 wagons to draw its deals and planks
    to the storage stacks
        like huddled apartments
    in rows like narrow streets around the mill
        its sawdust, its wooden beams and pillars
that anchor gangs of saws, log rollers
    log kickers, the grinders, the gantry crane
the bearings and choppers that rumble the wooden floor.

Booth sends his men from their posts to fight the flames
    fire reels wail in from every direction
        firemen haul their hoses through stinging smoke
        J. R in the thick at 73.

  *

Lost on LeBreton flats
    seven lives
    the homes of 8,000 people
    CPR's Broad Street Station
    the lying-in hospital called the House of Mercy
    the Bayswater Hotel
    the Post Office of Rochesterville and the general store
    and all that stood
        as far south as Dow's Lake.

Booth counts his losses:
    eight of the 200 horses around the mill
    six stables, 33,000 bushels of oats
    a wagon shop, paint shop, machine shop, blacksmith shop
    20 tenement houses
    his Duke Street office and papers
    the Preston Street house of his married daughter Gertrude
    and, across Preston Street

his own. Not a dormer remained.
　　Black cinders, broken walls open to sky. Close by
　　a chain of iron wheels
　　　　all that was left of a train.

　★　　　　　　　　　　　　　　　　　．

The sweet-bitter stink of charred wood
　　rises from the 400 acres of burn
　　whirls across the Upper Town to Parliament Hill
　　　　in gusts from the South
　　across the flat lands of Nepean farther than eye can see
　　　　when long blasts sweep from the North.

The wind carries stories:
　　the picture of Virgin Mary hung by a door
　　　　and the house was saved
　　the panicked horse that reared
　　　　and pulled a blazing beam onto its back
　　Hull families who fled northeast
　　to camp on the muddy shores of Lake Flora
　　　　cold feet and the smell of marsh
　　　　better than burning alive
　　crowding and fights in the shelters
　　　　mustered in ByWard Market and Lansdowne Park
　　the buckets of water dumped on Primrose Hill
　　　　to save the mansions of the rich.

Booth's sawmill stands above the ruins.
A mill hand wonders, did he hang a picture of himself outside?

Seared

J. R.

I cannot be quit of the roar of it
the shouts and coughs of the men
screams of the horses

my favourite lost, with the forehead
star and walleyes, the horse that always
stirred a hoof to greet me

the Apocalypse preached in the camp-meetings
of my youth, the End of Days before the Revelation —
crazy men, Father said

up from the States to make mischief.
My revelation: Frederick, the glad-hand,
lavish parties, wife dressed like a gypsy

the son who jokes with cullers, jobbers and trainmen
the length of the Valley, while stalwart
Jackson tends the daily accounts

protesting the sprinklers that Frederick
insisted be fastened on every wall at great expense
though none of the other mills took the step …

Sprinklers that kept the flames at bay,
sprinklers that Frederick invented.
Frederick, second son.

5

TALES TOLD

Tales from the Tavern on the Flats

Old John R. is leading the fight to shut the taverns.
Says he'll pay the city the licence fees.

> So a man don't have the right to drink his own pay!
> Enjoys a whiskey himself, they tell me.

> > A spoonful with dinner.

Drink to our barley repast!

> I mind the time he broke both legs
> jumping a ditch at the farm. Eighty if he was a day.
> Had his sons set the bones on the spot
> then went back to work.

> > … after a month or few.

Then there's the tale of the tip.

> Go ahead — We all like how you tell it.

Booth arrives at the lumber camp, see,
a man takes charge of his horse, and Booth
gives him a mighty 10-cent piece. Sez the hostler
Your son Jackson gives me a quarter. Sez Booth
He's the son of a rich man. I am an orphan.

> > I heard it was 25 cents and 50 cents.

> I heard 50 cents and a dollar.

> Remember the slick-suited lad
> looking for the old man in his office? He's out
> about the mill, sez the clerk. Lad
> tiptoes around in his fancy shoes, checks

through the lumber piles, the grading room,
finds a little man down in a pit, mixing mortar.
Please sir, can you direct me to Mr. Booth?
I'm Booth, sez the man in the pit.

Tale of the Shantyman's Wife

A tap at the door in the depths of night —
I tell you it gave me a start
me in my nightclothes, my husky woodsman
laid up I thought for his last, struck with pneumonia.

Mr. Booth himself stood at the door,
lantern in hand, red flannel draped over his arm.
May I come in, sez he, May I see him?
Asking! When we owe all we have to his wages.

I'd been praying to get Ewan through the night
his sweat soaking the pillow, me
blotting his forehead with towels, trying
to coax him to drink. Didn't Booth raise him up

with his own hands! Wrap him tight in that flannel
soaked with wine, sit in my bedside rocker the whole
night long. And just before dawn, didn't the fever
break! They tell me he sends away for medical

books and all manner of tinctures. A wonder
red flannel didn't help his wife — he never remarried
you know — or that poor girl, his youngest.
Twenty-three. Bless her soul.

In Which the Duchess of Cornwall and York Entertains Doubts about a Ride on the Timber Slide and Survives the Trip Accompanied by J. R. Booth

Amongst the experiences which the city offers to its visitors is the descent of the "slides," whereby the hardships of the lumberman's life become, for a few exciting moments, the attractive sport of the venturesome seekers of strange thrills ...

— F.A. DIXON, PICTURESQUE CANADA, TORONTO, 1882

What, I wonder aloud, should Royalty wear
     for a trip down a restless river?
On a conveyance called a crib?

It's easy for men: the Duke
will slip into a simple checked suit
with a black silk tie and a Derby.

His parents swear it was amusing.

Where, on a crib, does one plant the Royal standard?

Is a pork-and-bean luncheon
in a woodsman's shanty
an occasion one should anticipate
with pleasure?

        Think of it as a picnic, Your Highness,
        says my lady-in-waiting.

I would wish on such an occasion to do without stays.

        No, Ma'am, she says, tough hands
        tightening bone on bone.
        Not with a waist the envy of all.

        Even in this wild land, Ma'am
        the ladies vie for your style.
        White would have photographed well —
        pity we're in half-mourning

... the descent ... is made at a pace which, with the ever-present
possibility of a break-up, gives a very respectable sense of excitement
to a novice ... for a quarter of a mile appears a narrow channel, down
which a shallow stream of water is constantly rushing, with here and
there a drop of some five or eight feet; the ladies gather up their
garments ... At a bigger drop ... the water ... surges up through our
timbers and a shower of spray falls about us. A delicate "Oh!" from
the ladies ...

I hate to depart from the Royal trolley
crafted in Ottawa shops
and named after me.
Polished oak walls. Ceiling
veneered in bird's eye maple.
Such curtains! Carpet of royal blue.
Electric lamps!

But there is the windy river
and the Countess Minto insists.

Our craft a crude platform
small-parlour size — on this our party
must descend the slide? Not even sides
only a dais to keep us above the water
my seat of honour a wicker chair. Oh!
the stays pinch when I sit — my skirts
spill round condemned to drench.
A shorter hem would have served.

Booth points out a heron
stock-still on shoreline rock
long legs and beak
feathers draped like ermine —

the odd little white-beard — unrefined
of tongue and coat — is our host.
Everyone's favourite rough-hewn millionaire
whispers my husband's aide-de-camp.

Pushed off from shore we float at a hastening pace
toward the chute. I raise my gaze
to the timber gates, clutch my chair as the oarsmen
wield their sweeps, and over the edge
        we sway

                down the incline the logs the men crowds alongside
                    we race through sudden spray our host unfazed
                        hats wave Booth's blue eyes blaze
                            this is what matters the splash the speed
                                the dip
                            the bounce to calm.

Tale from the Feed Mill

This was before he was rich.
Starting out in Hull with a small plant
for shingles. He'd hitch up and carry a load,
sell it in Ottawa, then make the rounds for supplies.

So he comes to my mill for a quantity of fodder
finds he doesn't have cash to pay for it all.
I tell him, Go ahead, take what you need
— lord knows, he'd be good for the money.

Well sir. But a few minutes later, didn't he
wheel the horses back and return the part unpaid.
Couldn't unload fast enough. As if it would
burn through his wagon.

Horsepower

Phantoms sift through drifts
of morning mist. The clip-clop
of Booth's team on macadam
turns his brain to abacus.

Liveried chauffeur waiting, son Jackson
stalls beside his Silver Ghost, cigar
in hand. As if the car's a woman
he loves too much to rush.

Second son Frederick bought his Ghost first,
pearly cream. Its wraith-like silence glides
toward the mill. Frederick's glance caresses
the walnut dash, the fender's curve.

Daughter Gertrude's chauffeured Ghost
warms outside. She smooths her twill *tailleur*,
tugs kid fingers, will ride on dove-grey plush
to the day nursery board.

Dave Beauchard, long Booth's driver,
steeped in pipe smoke, old as he,
turns the buggy onto Albert Island.
At the office door, a final clop.

First to work again, says Booth,
and palms an equine haunch.
— Rolls Royce's 50 horse
can't match these two.

Tale of an Escape

Melt-flood from the Upper Ottawa
assaults the faltering cofferdam. Below,

a burly workman, intent on repair,
fails to spot the bulge

white-headed Booth sees from shore.
Downward Booth scramble-slips

cane and all, calling instructions unheard
like the foreman's cries that bounce

off his own mill-dimmed ears
as the dam-crack widens,

river-force surges, the foreman
grips Booth's arms, drags him back

from collapse of the whole
damned thing swept downstream.

Tangle of fragments.
Swirling man.

Tale of Two Fishing Sports, Rideau Club Lounge

Cigar?
We fitted him out with a rod and bait. He already had hip waders.

                              Is he not a member?

        Yes but he's never here.
        The river chilled right through the rubber.

But they were biting — bass, some nice perch.

        A muskie broke my line.

He stayed long enough to catch a good pickerel, but then he laid
rod on sand
and was off. Just for a minute, he claimed —
he'd spied a deadhead.

        Waterlogged wood — must have weighed ten stone
        but he dragged it out himself. Then disappeared.

We filled our creels, and when it was time to go we found him
around the point
beside a half-dozen salvaged logs.

        All bark-blazed with a turtle, mark you.

I got the better catch, says he.

Articles of Incorporation, 1921

A neat pile of papers, inkpot,
pen. The brass official seal.
With such I'm to cede
sole dominion
over my empire's heart.

My children and lawyer
        wait.

I've never let bankers
interfere, so why
after all these years
would I want to let lawyers
stick their fingers in?

                        Father, you're almost 94
                        says Frederick.
                        Even you
                        won't live forever.

Why not
I sometimes think — heart
strong, head clear, down at the mill
most days. Up in the pines
come fall.

                        Gertrude flicks her eyes
                        to Jackson
                        then Frederick.

Very well.
Where do you want me to sign?

Glimpsed at 96

What stooped white-beard,
trousers ankle-frayed, climbs
a lumber stack to thank dense crowds

of workmen for ninety-six cut
roses, long-stemmed, perfect,
as they have been every year?

6

A PLAIN MAN

Opeongo

—fall 1925, J.R.

Wafts of warmth from the *Opeongo's* steamheat.
Lamplight pooled on polished ceilings. Headquarters.
My spot on a Valley siding, which some
would call a stop on the way to nowhere.

Outside, the shanty farm has been put to bed for winter,
stripped fields grey and hard under the high cold moon.
How sweet the moonlight sleeps, Gertrude used to sing,
lines learned in Miss Harmon's School for Young Ladies

Shakespeare's works no part of my farm boy schooling
and not missed, my reading hours for newspapers —
Montreal, Boston, New York, Chicago.
Better I read of the present, look to the future. Tomorrow

I'll walk in the bosom of my forest. Talks at dawn
with my manager, plans for the season's cut. Again
I'll tread the needle-cushioned floor, breathe the tang
of pine, tonic for my blood these days gone sluggish.

Now my tall fur hat and matching fur-collared coat.
Clank of the metal stair down to track gravel.
Where are you going? cries Nurse Craig.
You'll catch your death!

Chilled stillness, breath a silver mist, stars
fine silver seeds sown across the dark
field of sky.

Dreams of Knights

J. R.

Nurse Craig reaches to close the blinds.
No, I say, I want to see out from my bed.
Rest, she says, rest. I insist, Not yet.

Shedding elms bend in wind. This morning
a hurdy-gurdy stopped by with a monkey,
set a-chatter my grandson and daughter-in-law.

Idle. I'm idle! Nurse Craig shushes me,
smooths my sheet. Idle like those foolish Knights
of Labor, who chose the time of a world recession

to ask for more. Disrupting the mills
to deprive of employment any child under 15.
Equal pay for women, they asked. A ten-hour day!

Times so bad every mill had to lower the weekly wage
by 50 cents. Winter coming — no pay, food more dear —
they should have worked and saved.

Instead they went on strike. Horses idle too. Idle!
Nurse Craig touches my wrist. I've been pounding,
she says, lowers the blinds so all I can look at

is the wooden shield on the arch that leads
to the hallway, meant for the crest
of my knighthood, unattained,

the title borne by my great-uncle
back in Ulster. I'd have had the honour
and money too.

Instead a blank shield —
monument to vain hopes.
Sleep calls. These days I cannot refuse.

John Rudolphus Booth 1827–1925

My family
knows my wishes.

Simple casket, no music,
no pallbearers, no flowers.
Service at home

in the oak-lined room
that has served me
these sixteen years.

A motor hearse
to my Beechwood rest
and the family
who passed before me.

I am a plain man.

December 9, 1925

Low grey skies a shroud
whipped by a fresh north wind.

On the frozen ground
between your house
and stable, a steel drum
where your records —
on your own mill's paper? —
smoulder
as you directed.
The last red ember
shrivels black.

December 11, 1925

MONARCH OF UPPER OTTAWA, FULL OF AGE, LAYS
DOWN HIS SCEPTER — *The Citizen*, Ottawa

Your house of stern
red brick. The heavy scent of roses.
Your family in its numbers
drawn from distances to mourn.

In the parlour where you lie
your three surviving children
— Jackson, Frederick, Gertrude —
and their families. Jackson's
wife Jesse, distraught. Jackson's son,
your youngest grandchild,
ultimately your heir — the lively boy
who sparked your tiring heart.
Cousins, half-brothers
nieces, grand-nephews. Miss Ora Craig,
your nurse and constant companion.

In the front room's bay,
your coffin: solid bronze
— why not pine? —
glass-topped for viewing.

Prime ministers present and past
crowd the family. A flourish
of diplomats climb
the steep front steps
between stone parapets
to the crepe-hung door.

Outside in bitter wind,
five thousand cram a city block,
until Jackson opens the house to all —

four abreast under the porte cochère,
in the side door to sign the memorial book,
names to be published
in the *Ottawa Evening Journal.*

Hundreds walk with the cortège.
Bystanders doff hats
despite the cold. Twenty Ottawa police
block traffic intrusions. Silence
from every Chaudière mill.

Six cars carry the flowers
you asked to do without

east on Sparks
past the newly closed-down
Russell House Hotel,
where a bold bid
founded your fortune,
down Rideau Street
past Sandy Hill where you built
Gertrude's new mansion
after the Great Fire.

Over your grave
red granite 20 feet tall,
a blanket of roses,
a ribbon inscribed
"Father."

Last Words, as Reported by Nurse Craig at the Interment

If I could have only one more walk
among the pines

I am sure I'd regain my strength.

Notes on the Poems

Kichi Sibi. "Calk boots" is pronounced "cork boots" and refers to the spike-soled boots worn by the river drivers to give them grip on floating logs.

Working the Limit. Limits were timber-cutting rights auctioned by the Crown. They applied to specific types and sizes of trees in a specific geographic area. At his peak in the 1890s J. R. Booth owned the largest expanse of limits in North America.

$45,000. A deal is a plank-like piece of lumber at least three inches thick. It is also, of course, a business agreement.

Tale of the Camboose Shanty Boy. The camboose or cambuse was a log fire that burned in the centre of a shanty, which was a rough shelter. Set in a log square filled with sand, the camboose provided light, heat, and cooking power. By extension, the term was applied to the shanty itself and to the whole cutting operation, men, horses, and provisions. It was also used for the cooking area, similar in structure, on a timber raft.

The Weaver's Tale. Found poem based on an article in *Sunset* magazine February 1917. Original text, minus selected words or phrases.

Why a Turtle? Booth's logs were marked on the bark with the symbol of a turtle. The cut ends were hammered with a diamond shape enclosing a stylized JB.

At the residence of her husband ... Details from the *Ottawa Evening Journal*, May 27 and 31 and the *Ottawa Daily Free Press*, May 29, 1886. Italicized portions are direct quotes.

In Which the Duchess ... The Duke and Duchess of Cornwall and York later became King George V and Queen Mary. His parents took a similar trip in 1870.

Opeongo. Booth's private railcar was built in Ottawa to luxurious Pullman standards. Booth used it as office and sleeping accommodation. Visiting dignitaries also used it, including Sir Wilfrid Laurier, who borrowed it for honoured guests.

Sources

Hurling Down the Pine, by John W. Hughson and Courtney C. J. Bond, The Historical Society of Gatineau, Old Chelsea, Quebec, 1965.

J. R. Booth, The Life and Times of an Ottawa Lumberking, John Ross Trinnell, Ottawa, TreeHouse Publishing, 1998.

The Lumberjacks, by Donald MacKay, McGraw-Hill Ryerson Limited, 1978. Source of epigraph to "Raftsmen," (Dickens quotation, from his "American Notes," 1842). Its first person accounts of shanty life animated poems about felling trees and delivering timbers and logs to market.

Lumber Kings and Shantymen, David Lee, James Lorimer & Company, Toronto, 2006. Prime source for information about mill technology.

Ottawa, An Illustrated History, John H. Taylor, James Lorimer and Company and Canadian Museum of Civilisation, Toronto 1986. Good source on the phases of the Ottawa Valley forest industry and its place in Ottawa's history.

The Private Capital: Ambition and Love in the Age of Macdonald and Laurier, Sandra Gwyn, McClelland and Stewart Limited, 1984.

Sisters in the Wilderness: The Lives of Susanna Moodie and Catharine Parr Traill, Charlotte Gray, Viking, Toronto, 1999.

*

"Booth, John Rudolphus," by Jamie Benidickson, *Dictionary of Canadian Biography*.

"The Booths of Ottawa," Doris French, a two-part article in Chatelaine magazine, December 1963 and January 1964. Prime source for poems about Booth's personal life.

"The John R. Booth Story," C. F. Coons, Ontario Department of Natural Resources, 1978.

"Canada's Lumber Interests and the Great Fire of 1900," Jon Fear, *Urban History Review / Revue d'Histoire Urbaine, June 1 1979*.

"The Canada Atlantic Railway," Wikipedia.

"Cleaning Up After the Log Drivers' Waltz," by Jamie Benidickson, in *Les Cahiers de droit*, Volume 51, Numéro 3-4, septembre–décembre 2010.

"Rivers of Sawdust," by R. Peter Gillis, in *Canadian Environmental History: Essential Readings*, ed. David Freeland Duke, Canadian Scholars Press, 2006. Source for the comment of Sir John A. Macdonald.

★

City of Ottawa Municipal Archives.

Historical Society of Ottawa Bytown Pamphlet Series.

Library and Archives Canada. Many photographs available online.

Ottawa Daily Free Press.

Ottawa Evening Journal.

Ottawa Evening Citizen.

Sessional Papers of the Dominion of Canada, Vol. 23.

Acknowledgements

With thanks to my husband Rick, whose interest in the
Ottawa Valley created a home library I've been able to pilfer,
and to the Ottawa Room of the Ottawa Public Library, the
Archives of the City of Ottawa, and the library of Carleton
University, whose resources I consulted but refrained from
pilfering. My gratitude to John H. Taylor and David Mullington
for exchanges about Booth's history, to Steven Brockwell,
Peter Levitt, and Susan Musgrave who got me hooked on
poetry, and to David O'Meara, Sawdust Reading Series,
Rhonda Douglas, and *Arc Poetry Magazine* for giving these
poems a giant boost when they needed it. Deep appreciation
to Blaine Marchand for casting his expert eye over the full
manuscript and Deanna Young for rescuing me from a slide
to discouragement. Thanks to the Thursday evening poets
with Shane Rhodes, and heartfelt thanks to my Ruby Tuesday
friends who were there from the start of this work with
encouragement, suggestions, and challenges.

To Robyn Sarah, whose meticulous, imaginative, and
good-humoured editing brought out the best in these poems:
thank you, thank you, thank you.

My appreciation to the editors of *Arc Poetry Magazine*, *Event*,
and *Ottawater*, in which some of these poems, in earlier versions,
first appeared.

About the Author

A lifelong resident of Ottawa, Jean Van Loon lives with her
Ottawa-born husband, not far from her two adult children
and an easy walk to the Ottawa River. Since retiring from
a career as a public servant and head of the steel industry's
national trade association, she has published poems and stories
in literary magazines across Canada. When not at her desk,
she often walks through the Experimental Farm, comprised in
large part of farmland bought from J. R. Booth. *Building on River*
is her first book-length publication.